Serenity
in a Garden

by

Judy Carlson

Balboa Press books may be ordered through booksellers or by contacting:

Balboa Press
A Division of Hay House
1663 Liberty Drive
Bloomington, IN 47403
www.balboapress.com
1 (877) 407-4847

Because of the dynamic nature of the Internet, any web addresses or links contained in this book may have changed since publication and may no longer be valid. The views expressed in this work are solely those of the author and do not necessarily reflect the views of the publisher, and the publisher hereby disclaims any responsibility for them.

Any people depicted in stock imagery provided by Thinkstock are models, and such images are being used for illustrative purposes only.
Certain stock imagery © Thinkstock.

ISBN: 978-1-4525-9751-5 (sc)
ISBN: 978-1-4525-9752-2 (e)

Library of Congress Control Number: 2014920232

Printed in the United States of America.

Balboa Press rev. date: 11/26/2014

BALBOA.
PRESS
A DIVISION OF HAY HOUSE

Serenity
in a Garden

by

Judy Carlson

Also: "Reflections from a Garden"
"Life Lessons from a Garden"

"In the Garden"

I come to the garden alone
While the dew is still on the roses
And the voice I hear falling on my ear
The Son of God discloses.

Refrain:
And He walks with me, and He talks with me,
And He tells me I am His own;
And the joy we share as we tarry there,
None other has ever known.

He speaks, and the sound of His voice,
Is so sweet the birds hush their singing,
And the melody that He gave to me
Within my heart is ringing.

Refrain:
And He walks with me, and He talks with me,
And He tells me I am His own;
And the joy we share as we tarry there,
None other has ever known.

I'd stay in the garden with Him
Though the night around me be falling,
But He bids me go; through the voice of woe
His voice to me is calling. Austin Miles, 1912

It was a cold winter here in the high desert of Nevada. The nights brought freezing temperatures to the rose garden. The result was that several of my beautiful roses could not overcome the deep cold. I wonder what in my life brings a deep cold and how do I warm my heart and soul?

If you chose life then you must also make a decision to support that choice. My life experience has taught me that the dying and rising moments pass, but what remains are the lessons you learn. Behind every face there runs a mini-series fit for the story telling on TV. I never wanted to be stuck in one place. The context of journeying is movement and I wanted forward movement. We all share in the journey; we all share in the story.

"Whatever is lovely … think about such things…"

Philippians 4:8

So it is attitude that I have most worked on in my third and last trimester of life. I watched the newscasts this morning and realized that the world's crises are far and away beyond me. It could overwhelm a person but this is what I do and I share in the hope that what has worked for me will also work for one of you. I can only care for, love, be generous, forgive and serve what is in my life. I have come to realize that we are all connected in this exquisite universe and no prayer or act of love or kindness ever goes to waste. We are not all called to change the world in huge ways but we are all called to love.

"This is my commandment: love one another as I have loved you."

John 15:12

"I come to the Garden alone while the dew is still on the roses …"
"In the Garden" by Austin Miles

Opening Night

This rose is named Opening Night, and I try to always be open to what comes in life. What if the life lessons you experience are specifically ordained for you? What if they are tailor made? What if instead of running and hiding you walk head long into what comes? What if being open to what you can learn changes the outcome or at least lessens the stress? Sometimes we have to settle for questions with no promise of an answer. I go outside, into my garden…

"Be still, and know that I AM God!"
Psalm 46:11

Perfume Delight

Smell, it is a wonderful sense. We can smell chocolate chip cookies in the oven, a turkey dinner on Thanksgiving, the scent of pine as we decorate the Christmas tree, and the heavenly scent of roses. It must be very important to us for billions of dollars are spent on cologne, both for men and women.

All of these scents trigger more than the olfactory. They trigger memories; they call us to another place and time.

I am so called in my garden. The perfume drifts up from the roses as you walk among them. It enhances the sense of peace in the garden. It is one more gift that the garden gives.

"He said to Simon, Do you see this woman? You did not anoint my head with oil, but she anointed my feet with perfume....and He said to the woman, your faith has saved you go in peace."
Luke 7:44- 50

Princess Grace de Monaco

This rose is both beautiful and elegant. It is named for Grace Kelly. The name grace means patient and as I read up on the origins of this rose I am delighted that I practiced patience with it. They intended to add a strong immune system to this delicate looking rose, to make it disease resistant, but in all honesty I must say it was afflicted with several problems.

It was the first rose of the season to become ill. Its problems were communicable so as I treated it, I treated all around. The battle for its beauty was well fought. It definitely responded to care and now once again graces my garden. I believe that it is healthy to be patient with yourself. God's grace does not fall from heaven periodically. It surrounds and embraces the world every moment.

"Yet He gives grace to the afflicted"
Proverbs 3:34

Neptune

What comes to your mind when you think of the heavens? I think of *Psalm 14:2. " The Lord has looked down from heaven upon the sons of men, to see if there are any who understand, who seek after God."* The Neptune rose takes me to the heavens not just because it makes me think of the planet but because of the color. Apparently, when you see Neptune through a telescope it has a soft purple glow because of its clouds. Some say that science and faith in God are incompatible, but I see science as the study of God, the creation seeking to find the creator. The stars and the planets and what lie far beyond our telescopes are but the fingerprint of God.

"When I consider Thy heavens, the work of Thy fingers
the moon and the stars which Thou hast ordained,
What is man that Thou dost take thought of him?"
Psalm 8:4,5

Lark Ascending

This apricot English rose has petals that cup to hold mercy. The Lark Ascending is a poem written by George Meredith in 1881. It is about the song of the skylark.

> "Renew'd in endless notes of glee
> So thirsty of his voice is he,
> For all to hear and all to know,
> That he is joy, awake, aglow…"

I am always faithful to feed the birds in my garden. They bring song and activity, and as I wrote about in my previous book, *Reflections from a Garden*, joy as they splash about together bathing. The mercies of God are new every morning and I believe that if we open our hearts and souls like the cup petals of the Lark Ascending rose we will be able to be awash in God's love. Let your Spirit soar and meet God's mercy as it falls - new every morning.

> *"The Lord's loving kindnesses indeed never cease, for His compassion never fails.*
> *His mercies are new every morning, so great is His faithfulness …"*
> Lamentations 3:22,23

Remember Me

This rose was bred in Scotland and it was bred to be a hardy rose as the winds blowing off the North Sea are cold and brisk. It has been chosen as a representative rose for the Remember Me rose gardens that will be planted at all of the 9/11 memorial sites. It was said that churches of every denomination were full after that terrible tragedy. We fell to our knees as a nation trying to come to terms with that intensity of hatred. I believe that when we remember we are in times past.

Since I spend so much time in my garden I sought definitions of time. Philosophers offer differing views on the nature of time. Newtonian time says that it is a structure of the universe and a dimension in which events occur in sequence. An opposing view is that time is neither an event nor a thing and thus cannot be measured nor travelled. However, when I remember a person or event in the past am I not bringing them into the present? We all carry people and events in our hearts.

"There is an appointed time for everything, and a time for every event under the heavens. A time to give birth, and a time to die; a time to plant and a time to harvest... a time to tear down and a time to build. A time to weep and a time to laugh; a time to mourn and a time to dance…."
Ecclesiastes 3:1-4

Sunshine Daydream

Sunshine Daydream is such a happy welcoming color and very faithful to be stunning in the morning. This rose is an heirloom rose. In the quiet of the morning I will worship God's name. I will lift my voice to praise Him. I chose to be in my garden because to me it is holy ground. It is where I can remove my shoes and seek the living God. I go out to look for Him among the beautiful ways in which He leaves clues to His nature. I see God in the colors; in the lovely delicate forms of the flowers; I hear him in the sounds; and I sense Him in the fragrance of the roses and the earth. I see, feel, and hear the miracles of the universe unfolding before me.

"For your love is better than life: my lips shall glorify you.
Thus will I bless You while I live; lifting up my hands, I will call upon Your name."
Psalm 63:4-5

Koko Loco

This is such a unique rose. It buds as a mild chocolate brown and opens in shades of light lavender. It is transformed. We too are transformed in life. We move through stages of dying and rising, discovering and letting go. The difficulties that we face ultimately form us in strength and wisdom. How can we know the exhilaration and joy of success without the pains of testing? When I received the diagnosis of a rare type of blood disorder I was fearful and panicked. I decided to make the best of every moment that I had left and for me that meant going outside. I followed my heart and it led to a garden. I was able to connect with the beauty and it brought me great joy.

"And not only this but we also exult in our tribulations, knowing that tribulation brings about perseverance, and perseverance proven character, and proven character hope, and hope does not disappoint, because the love of God has been poured out within our hearts...."
Romans 5:3,4,5

Double Delight

This rose mingles the colors of white and a strawberry red. I see Double Delight as an invitation to abundance. "And so, as those who have been chosen of God, holy and beloved, put on a heart of compassion, kindness, humility, gentleness and patience; bearing with one another, and forgiving each other... and let the peace of Christ rule in your hearts" (Colossians 3:12,13).

If we want to know what the will of God is for us, we need look no further than the Word of God - the Bible. No matter which human condition you find yourself in; no matter what human condition I find my self in, I chose to love God. I chose to sit in the garden where peace rules in my heart and be grateful. I chose to put compassion in my heart and kindness, humility and gentleness. The garden is a perfect place for me to meditate on these virtues and how, when, and with whom I can practice them. It is not enough to read, but for the Word to be living and active it must take on flesh. When we place these virtues on our lips and then in our minds and hearts it is only a first step. The fulfillment is when our hands and feet bring these virtues alive into the world.

"Christ has no body now on earth but yours
no hands but yours, no feet but yours
Yours are the eyes through which He looks
with compassion on the world
yours are the feet with which He goes about doing good
Yours are the hands,
with which He blesses all the world"
Saint Theresa of Avila

Bewitched

The definition of bewitched is to be put under a spell or to be influenced by magic. As with all things I believe there is shadow and light to everything. I remember hearing a grandmother say that her granddaughter was 'magical'. I understood her meaning. The child was so very beautiful and sweet as to be otherworldly. It strikes to the very heart of one of our greatest gifts from God - our free will. We have the ability to transform our lives and loved ones by reframing our experiences. We can chose. You may very well have a power that you are unaware of. I will give you an example of reframing an experience. I had a dear friend who was very ill and dying. She was frightened by death because she had a sister who pre-deceased her who appeared to be shocked before she passed away. When a long time precious friend came to be with her, he suggested that they reframe the sister's experience. The alternate explanation could have been that the other sister, as she was dying, saw a glimpse of heaven or another relative long gone. Would that not explain also the shocked look? This new way of looking at it comforted my friend and allowed her a peaceful passing.

So be grounded in this beautiful earth but always look up! When your eyes see only the goodness of God in the beauty of nature it brings magic into your day.

"Set your minds on the things above …."
Colossians 3:2

Sugar Moon

The moon is the most luminous object in the sky after the sun. Since ancient times the moon has influenced us. There are hundreds of songs about the moon. "Fly me to the Moon," "Carolina Moon," "Moon River," "Moonlight Becomes You," "Moonshadow," and "Shine on Harvest Moon" are just a very few. Then there are the classical pieces "Moonlight Sonata" by Beethoven and Debussey's "Clair de Lune." We are fascinated by the heavens. We see in the heavens the elegance and majesty of the Creator, and the soul sings.

This pure white rose has such a sweet fragrance it may actually smell of heaven. I have two of them in my garden this year and they both survived a very cold winter here in Northern Nevada. The moon seems to have a subtle power over us or at least a fascination. When we pause to actually notice the rare beauty all around us we are glorifying God.

"The heavens are telling of the glory of God …."
Psalm 19:1

New Year

This rose was bred in New Zealand in1983. It has three distinct colors in its petals: yellow, crimson and orange. The colors are best displayed when the flower opens. The outer petals tend to roll down exposing the whole flower. It is a true natural example of the beauty of the soul. The rose reaches the pinnacle of its beauty after it fully opens. I would have to say that this rose is the most photogenic of all 50 in my garden. When I see a flower or the petals of a rose turned down I think of humility and then service. They are partners; one flowing seamlessly out of the other. We are made new every time we set ourselves aside to encourage the wellbeing of another. It is soul work, as we all know, the ego only seeks its own.

"For you were called to freedom, brothers. Only do not use your freedom as an opportunity for the flesh, but through love serve one another. For the whole law is fulfilled in one word: You shall love your neighbor as yourself."
Galatians 5:13-14

Elizabeth

Elizabeth is not a new rose in my garden, however as I had two of them I am now down to this one. If I may be gender sensitive I will say that everything about Elizabeth is lovely, delicate and feminine. The name Elizabeth is Hebrew for "Oath of God."

It is that God thought of us that we exist at all, and we are sustained by His love for us. He conceived of us before we were conceived in our Mothers.

There is much meaning in a name. Throughout scripture names matter and are sometimes changed to illustrate the transformation of the person. Abram became Abraham, Simon became Peter, and Sarai became Sarah. I believe that God whispers our name into our soul as life begins. It is the most intimate of acts, sharing breath with us. We are told in scripture to lay up our treasure in heaven and also that there is the promise of a new heavenly name.

"Whoever has ears ought to hear what the Spirit says…
to him who overcomes…
I will give him a white stone, and a new name written on the stone
which no one knows but he who receives it."
Revelation 2:17

Sundowner

This rose is a golden orange with touches of salmon. It has a very pleasant fragrance. It is sold as a bare root rose. That means that it was just a root ball and a few canes when I purchased it. It was a bold move to buy a rose of this kind with our unpredictable spring weather. The high desert of Nevada can be lovely and sunny during the day and yet bring us a nighttime frost.

There is in Spencer, Massachusetts an order of Trappist Monks who live a contemplative life, dedicating themselves to the praise and worship of God in a hidden way. Following the sixth century Rule of St. Benedict, they live in silence and solitude, prayer and penitence. The monks generate praise and worship ascending to God from the rising of the sun to its setting. It is in our American nature to work hard, to move, to be productive. To be still and wholly enter the now takes practice. In the garden it becomes easier to sit among the flowers see their colors and smell their perfume and think of God's goodness.

"From the rising of the sun to it's setting
the name of the Lord is to be praised."
Psalm 113:3

Golden Shower

This is a beautiful fragrant yellow climber. Golden Shower was also planted as a bare root rose. I must say that I have always been afraid of heights. When I was a little girl I dreaded the teeter-totter because if the other stopped low to the ground, it meant that I was the one up in the air. The foot or so I was off the ground was too much. Now though, the thought of climbing to the heavens appeals to me. Do not let fear be the primary motivator in your life.

"Jacob went into a deep sleep and began to dream and behold, a ladder was set on the earth with its top reaching to heaven; and behold, the angels of God were ascending and descending on it."
Genesis 28:12

Brother Cadfael

This rose has giant blooms with the look of a peony. It is one of the reasons that I initially resisted planting the David Austin roses in my garden. This one I have planted by the arbor that my son, KC, made for me. My hope is that it will climb and cover the arbor with its huge pink flowers.

As I followed my heart outside and into the garden the quiet enveloped me. I began to notice that I was using my five senses in new ways. The breeze would brush against my face carrying the scent of the rose perfume. Was I feeling or smelling? The beauty of the roses was so overwhelming to me that it felt like my eyes were in my heart not my head.

These were all new experiences. The more I lived in the moment the more I understood.

I also want to recommend to you that you enjoy a good read while you are in the garden. The mysteries of Brother Cadfael, the namesake of this rose, are set in eleventh century England. There are 20 books in the series. Take a book with you or a journal and enjoy your time in the garden.

Winchester Cathedral

This gorgeous, old English rose has a mass of flowers and has bloomed for me continuously all summer. It has become one of my very favorite roses. It is named in honor of Winchester Cathedral in Winchester, England. The cathedral is man's attempt to make a place for God to dwell on the earth, as David did in biblical times. The present church dates back to 1079. Its structure is very unique and reflects the architecture popular in its day. It is full of history; among those characters buried there are Saints and Kings and even Vikings.

I believe that it is a glorious thing to make a space for God in our lives. Jesus made it clear that we no longer need the Holy of Holies where only the high priest can enter. We only need call on His name with a sincere heart.

"But who is able to build a house for Him, for the heavens and the highest heavens cannot contain Him?"
2Chronicles 2:5

About Face

This is not a new rose in my garden but it is faithful and lovely. It is a grandiflora rose and somewhat unique for the changes in color it undergoes. We too undergo changes in color. It opens to a core of a bronze orange and lightens as its petals open. The fragrance is even very distinct. I think we burn brightly in our youth. We have so much energy and enthusiasm for the future. We can't wait to experience everything life has to offer. As we grow throughout our journey we mellow and learn growing in wisdom, grace, patience and peace. It took illness for me to change colors, to view the world differently. Blindness is one of the maladies most addressed by the Lord. Some might think that my health problems were a negative thing in my life but …

"We know that all things work together for good for those who love the Lord and are called according to His purpose"
Romans 8:28

Fragrant Cloud

This rose is such an unusual color. I was hard pressed to decide whether it was in the pink family or an orange with a hint of red. What I can tell you after nurturing it all summer long is how very gorgeous it is. I selected this rose not for the color, but for its name. I love to look up at the Nevada sky; we have such clear, clean blue skies. There is plenty of life in the sky to admire. I feed the birds and have so many varieties coming for breakfast and dinner. I must admit that I have been amazed at how they all get along. The larger birds like the robins and yellow-headed blackbirds seem content to allow the little finches and sparrows a pass.

Living out in the country by ranches also draws my eyes to the sky. On the breezy days you can see above the fields the hawks riding the wind, being lifted up higher and higher.

I can't help imagining what it must be like to be so free. I took my dog outside tonight and as always looked up at the sky. The clouds had broken up into feather-like wisps. So, today as I am writing about Fragrant Cloud, the Nevada sky is full of affirmation.

"And another angel came and stood at the altar, holding a golden censor and much incense was given to him, that he might add it to the prayers of all the saints…"
Revelation 8:3

Moonstone

Here we are back in the heavens with this rose. This gem is a very large pure white rose that has a delicate touch of pink inside. Once again we have fortitude residing in the disguise of frailty. I can testify to the vigor of this rose as we have endured a very hot and dry summer this 2014. Moonstone has everything to be beautiful in a Nevada garden. Its look of porcelain is surreal.

The moon is another gift from God, placed in the sky to be a night light. The moon and the stars are for those who look up. The moon cycles through phases as do we in our lives. We are all each and every one of us part of this glorious creation and we journey together whether we are always aware of it or not. When I received a diagnosis of a rare illness I was shaken to the core, shaken awake. I see in nature, in all creation, the imprint of an all-loving God.

"To Him who made the great lights, for His lovingkindness is everlasting,
the sun to rule by day….the moon and stars to rule by night….
For His lovingkindness is everlasting."
Psalm 136:7,8,9

Wild Blue Yonder

This ruby red and purple rose has clusters of ruffled petals. It is so perfect for our area of Nevada, it is almost shameful for me to write about. It could have been named more appropriately for the wild blue of the Nevada sky. We have a military station here where on any given day you can hear the sound of freedom over head.

"Up, up the long, delirious, burning blue
I've topped the wind-swept heights with easy grace.
Where never lark, or even eagle flew ...."
"High Flight" by John Magee

Purple Tiger

What a great name for a rose and what a dramatically colored bloom! The petals, each one, are a rich shade of purple with streaks and flecks of white. It is a very impressive addition to the garden. It has a strong and powerful look but it actually barely survived our Nevada winter nights. The reflection that I take from Purple Tiger is that even though we, me, all people, can cover their tenderness with a facade of confidence and bold color, we are all really truly vulnerable. We all need to be loved and forgiven and appreciated, and, yes, respected.

"Love is a fruit in season at all times, and within reach of every hand."
Mother Teresa

"We have been created for greater things. Not just to be a number in the world, not just to go for diplomas and degrees, this work and that work. We have been created in order to love and be loved."
Mother Teresa

Betty Boop

I admit this rose will not be easy to wax eloquent (assuming you think that I have so far) upon but it is so fun, I simply have to include it. This rose is bright and beautiful and full of colorful blooms. If you don't have something in your garden to make you smile, I recommend that you go plant something to serve that purpose. The current data on boosting your immune system includes laughter, fruits and vegetables, and even singing. I of course recommend doing what your medical provider advises also. This book, however, is about my garden making such a huge difference in my attitude, outlook and mindset, and therefore my health. Be light hearted and of good cheer, the world is a beautiful place.

"Trust in the Living God who gives us richly all things to enjoy."
1Timothy 6:17

Peace

This is one of those roses that can take your breath away. I am not the first person to see in the rose a metaphor for life. The incredible beauty, its colors and the softness of the petals, and how delicate and sensitive it can be. My roses require attention to thrive, love as it were. The more time you are able to spend with them the greater the reward in terms of their performance and beauty. The huge variety of color and type are similar to humanity.

However, along with the delicacy and beauty existing on the same rose are thorns. There is opportunity for injury. The chemo medicine that I take thins my blood so every time I approach without caution I am pricked and I bleed. It is not just me who can suffer for a wrong move in the garden. The wind here in northern Nevada can whip my rose garden into a dance, but as they move the thorns damage the bush. They are responsible for their own injury. Can the same not be said of us?

"Peace I leave with you, My peace I give to you."
John 14:27

Pink Iceberg

This rose is a certainty in my garden. It endured our coldest nights and now makes an offering of huge numbers of blooms. Truly it is a little showstopper. It apparently does just as well if potted, so if you are restricted from caring for a larger rose garden this rose bush is for you. My intention in writing, *Reflections from a Garden* and now this second volume is to encourage and inspire you. My journey of illness took me on a path outside to a garden. I want you to know that you are not alone, that we all journey together in some respect. We are fearfully and wonderfully made but that is no guarantee of perfect health for a life span. I pray and wish for you who read this book that life's challenges will never get you down. That you will go into the quiet, reach deep inside, and find hope and live it everyday.

"For I know the plans I have for you declares the Lord, plans for welfare, to give you a future, and for hope."
Jeremiah 29:11

Show Biz

I think that this rose is more Show Off than Show Biz. You have to love a character that strives to be the very best that God created it to be, and that is the example of this rose for me. I admit that this is a difficult lesson from the garden - to be the best you, everyday.

"And be kind to one another, tenderhearted, forgiving each other, just as God in Christ also has forgiven you ..."
Ephesians 4:32

Rainbow Sorbet

Scripture describes how God told Noah that He was establishing a perpetual covenant, the making of the rainbow. "And God said: 'This is the sign of the covenant which I make between Me and you, and every living creature that is with you, for perpetual generations: I set My rainbow in the clouds, and it shall be the sign of the covenant between Me and the earth" (Genesis 9:12-13). The rainbow is one of the most beautiful reminders in the sky of hope. The covenant differs from contract in that it is similar to a family bond. We are a huge family - all connected to each other and all living with the same heart. What I most love about this scripture is that the covenant is with every living creature for perpetual generations. Truly Good News!

Lasting Love

This rose is new this year in my garden. It is a lovely dusty red with a powerful fragrance. Once again I selected this rose for my garden not because of its color but for the name. My husband and I are approaching our 45th wedding anniversary this summer and lasting love is on my mind. There is no lovelier treatise on Love than 1 Corinthians 13.

"Love is patient, love is kind, it is not jealous, love does not brag and is not arrogant,
does not act unbecomingly; it does not seek its own, is not provoked, does not brood
over wrongs, does not rejoice over unrighteousness but rejoices with the truth.

Love bears all things, believes all things, hopes all things, endures all things. LOVE NEVER FAILS."
1 Corinthians 13:4 (emphasis added)

Ketchup and Mustard

5/15/2014 6:12

This rose is certain to become a favorite in any garden. It has layers of the brightest red placed on the backside of darkest yellow. It is bold and beautiful. It makes me ask what do I add to my life to spice it up? Well, obviously I spend time in my garden, not just enjoying nature but being grateful for it's gifts. I find it a comfort to connect with God and it seems so much easier to live the connection in the garden. I identify with the struggle of being the best me while meeting life's challenges. I see scripture come alive.

"For the word of God is living and active and sharper than any two-edged sword, and piercing as far as the division of soul and spirit, of both joints and marrow, and able to judge the thoughts and intentions of the heart."
Hebrews 4:12

Charlotte

Charlotte has exquisite cup-shaped petals of a medium size. It is a soft yellow color.

It was dedicated to Charlotte, who is one of David Austin's granddaughters. You can prune it to a bush, but it will also grow as a climbing rose. I appreciate its diversity. I know from my 65 years that being flexible of spirit is a quality that always enhances peace.

Have you considered the possibility of dedicating your husband, children, family, home, friends, work, pets, your life to God? It is He who first loved us. When we open a gift, do we not immediately thank the giver? Do we not honor the gift by using it or giving it a place of importance in our lives? I will be the first to admit that I take my days for granted and everything that God has filled them with.

"If it does not please you to serve the Lord, decide today whom you will
serve…as for me and my household, we will serve the Lord."
Joshua 24:15

Snowfire

Snow and fire are two seemingly incompatible elements wrapping around each other to create beauty. I find that life in the garden is exactly this principle. The beautiful scents from the roses, the softness to the touch of their petals, the exquisite colors as they perform, and yet the struggles and assaults to their nature waiting for an opportunity. The hundred-degree heat and intense sunshine of four thousand feet above sea level; the spider mites; the aphids; the powdery mildew; and the black spot all taking their turn to assault. One might wonder, is it worth the battle?

I write to tell you that it is indeed worth the fight. Whatever the life circumstance you find yourself in, we all experience triumph and tragedy, dying and rising. But what matters is how you journey through life. It took serious illness to wake me up. In the quiet and beauty of nature I began to see that we are all connected. We all play our part and we all matter greatly.

"For I am convinced that neither death, nor life, nor angels, nor principalities, nor present things, nor future things, nor powers, nor height, nor depth, nor any other creature will be able to separate us from the love of God in Christ Jesus our Lord."
Romans 8:38,39

Pope John Paul 2

I believe it is fitting that this gorgeous pure white rose is dedicated to Pope John Paul. When he was a college freshman he fought the anti-Semitic policies of his school. Until the Nazis closed the university, he aided a Jewish student about campus by protecting her from anti-Semitic bullies. What moved him was his heart for humanity. John Paul has said he grew up knowing that Jews and Christians prayed to the same God. He became the first pope since St. Peter to preach in a synagogue.

"Hear oh Israel the Lord is our God, the Lord is one!"
Deuteronomy 6:4

Easy Does It

It is easy to stay in the garden all day. Truthfully though, it is work to encourage flowers to thrive at this altitude and in the heat of our desert summer. The challenge makes the reward all the sweeter.

The rose Easy Does It, is a blend of mango-orange, peach-pink, and ripe apricot colors. It is a hardy rose and will continue to bloom all summer long. The lovely flowers of this rose attract butterflies and bees. I love having diversity in the garden. To sit outside with my dog Coco and a cup of coffee in the morning; to watch the birds come to bathe and have breakfast; to connect with God and tell of all the blessings I am grateful for. To give thanks for all that has been, all that is, and all that will be.

"I am the Alpha and the Omega, the first and the last, the beginning and the end. Blessed are those who wash their robes, so that they may have the right to the tree of life, and may enter by the gates into the city."
Revelation 22:13,14

Moonlight Magic

So here I am back with the Moon. The moon roses have featured beautifully in my garden. They obviously inspire and take people to the heavens.

"When I consider Thy heavens, the moon and the stars which Thou hast ordained;
What is man that Thou dost take thought of him?"
Psalm 8:4,5

Brandy

This Brandy rose may well be the most delicious rose in my garden. It is easy to linger over its color, form and fragrance. There are some things in life that exist purely to be beautiful and this rose is one of them. The gifts in nature are always there for the taking if we only have eyes to see. It is apricot in color and in our warmer climate it promises to have huge blooms.

I was hard pressed to make room in my garden for Brandy, I already had 50 roses to care for. I dug a little corner in the back, next to the house not aware of the quality of this rose. Sometimes the best and most beautiful things in our lives are overlooked.

"Do you have eyes and not see…"
Mark 8:18

Legends

Oprah Winfrey was involved in the final selection of the Legends rose. It was chosen to pay tribute to women who were honored during Oprah's Legends Weekend. A legend can be a story from the past that may or may not be true or a person who is revered for being exceptional. The bloom on this beautiful, red rose is exceptional in that it is much larger than any other in my garden. I want to reflect on the soul with this last rose. The soul is defined differently by all religious denominations but I do not write to be religious. I only know it is that innermost aspect of humans that is of great value and in so many ways remains mysterious. This Legends rose has qualities that put me in mind of a soul. I see in it generosity, kindness and complete humility. It opens fully and is vulnerable in its giving. There is abundance. The beauty is profound with no pride. The soul within you is your authentic self. It is a journey of a lifetime to discover that beauty within you but well worth the travel, as the Jesuit priest Pierre Teilhard de Chardin said: "We are spiritual beings on a human journey." Paul tells us the mystery held back for ages and ages that:

"God willed to make known what is the riches of the glory of this mystery
among the Gentiles, which is Christ in you, the hope of glory."
Colossians 1:27, 28

The Nevada Sky

So I end my garden tour with a picture of an evening sky. The Nevada sky is clear, clean, and bright blue. It is a perfect canvas for inspiring sights. These small wispy clouds looked like feathers somehow tossed against the blue. I encourage you to have eyes to see the beauty all around. Take the time to look, love and be grateful.

"Seek God, but once you find him it will send you on a search of never finding Him."
Saint Augustine

Salt Grass

This is obviously not one of my roses, but it has a life lesson to draw from. These blades of grass have pushed their way through asphalt. These tender sticks of grass one at a time have made their way through tar and rock.

Tenacious…persistent….

"I have fought the good fight, I have finished the course, I have kept the faith."
2Timothy 4:7

Judy Carlson lives in Fallon Nevada with her husband of 45 years, Kurt Carlson. They were both originally Canadian; she born in Sarnia Ontario, and he in Cornwall Ontario. They immigrated into Indiana in 1976, eventually moving west and making their home in Fallon. They raised three sons and have five dogs among them, Coco, Boo, Tango, Dulcinea and Rocinante.

Acknowledgements:

For my friend and Spiritual Mentor, Lawrence Quilici. He has always been honest with me without being hurtful. He has always encouraged me to be the best soul that I can be. He has always inspired me. He is a wonderful man.

For my family, for their loving support and constant encouragement. I have had the privilege of living out my life with wonderful men.

The Nurseries of "Flower Tree" and "J and K Llamas" played no small part in my love for gardening. I thank them for their vocation of bringing beauty to the world.

Your Thoughts

Your Thoughts

Your Thoughts

Your Thoughts

Printed in the United States
By Bookmasters